B is for Buckeye

An Ohio Alphabet

To Brigid —
Enjoy Ohio —
from a to Z!
Marcia Schonberg

Written by Marcia Schonberg and Illustrated by Bruce Langton

Photo reference for the letter D provided by Hemera.
Photo references for the letters C, G, H, M, U, and Z provided through the photography
of Marcia Schonberg.

Sleeping Bear Press
310 North Main Street
Chelsea, MI 48118
www.sleepingbearpress.com

Sleeping Bear Press is an imprint of The Gale Group, Inc.

Printed and bound in Canada.

10 9 8 7 6 5 4

Library of Congress Cataloging-in-Publication Data
Schonberg, Marcia.
B is for buckeye: an Ohio alphabet / by Marcia Schonberg.
p. cm.
ISBN: 1-58536-004-X
1. Ohio–Juvenile literature. 2. English language–Alphabet–Juvenile literature. [1. Ohio.
2. Alphabet.] I. Title.
F491.3 .S36 2000
977.1–dc21   00-010979

For Brandon and Joel
Adam, David, Lisa, and Jeff—
With special gratitude to Bill, who so lovingly inspires us all.

—Marcia Schonberg

My thanks go out to my parents
for giving me faith and inspiration to be an artist.

My love goes out to my wife Rebecca
and my children Brett and Rory
for being by my side and understanding my desires and dreams.

My gratitude to Sleeping Bear Press and
Marcia Schonberg in helping to make those dreams come true.

—Bruce G. Langton

A is for Astronauts
speeding through space.
They circle the earth and walk on the moon,
exploring a dark and exciting place.

Ohio has produced more astronauts than any other state. Twenty-three Ohioans have flown into outer space, among them John Glenn, who rocketed into the atmosphere aboard the *Friendship 7* on February 20, 1962, to become the first American to circle the earth—and he did it three times. After retiring from the National Aeronautics and Space Administration (NASA), he entered Ohio politics and in 1974 and 1980 was elected to the U.S. Senate. When John Glenn flew into outer space in 1998 aboard the *Discovery*, he became the oldest person to make a space flight.

With people all around the world breathlessly watching TV sets on July 20, 1969, Neil Armstrong became the first person to walk on the moon.

Kathryn Sullivan, who flew aboard the *Challenger* in October 1984, was the first U.S. woman to walk in outer space.

In July 1995, a five-person team flew in the shuttle *Discovery* to launch satellites into outer space. Only one of those five adventurers was not an Ohioan, so Governor George Voinovich made Kevin Kregel an honorary citizen of our state to make this an all-Ohio team.

Aa

Ohio is known as the Buckeye State because Buckeye trees grow so abundantly here. William Henry Harrison, the ninth U.S. President, helped introduce the Buckeye to the country in the nineteenth century. Although he was born in Virginia to a wealthy family, during his election year in 1839, Harrison was pictured as a down-to-earth western farmer. Stories claimed that he was born in a log cabin built of the Buckeye tree. In the nation's eyes the connection between Ohio and Buckeye was launched.

Dawes Arboretum in Newark has the "Famous 17"—Buckeye trees planted in the shape of the number 17—as a reminder that in 1803 Ohio became the 17th state to enter the Union.

Native Americans called the shiny brown Buckeye seed "hetuck," meaning "the eye of the buck," because it reminded them of a male deer's eye. The tree can grow to 100 feet in height. Its leaves are large and shaped like palms, with long, showy flower spikes, and large, prickly nuts containing inedible kernels, or buckeyes.

B is for Buckeye,
Ohio's nickname and tree.
Its nut looks like a deer's eye,
early pioneers would all agree.

From the day it was founded, Columbus has had as many adventures as its daring namesake, Christopher Columbus. The first settlers arrived here in 1797. When Ohio became the 17th state, Chillicothe was named the first state capital, but when farmers in the heart of Ohio offered 1,200 acres of land and $50,000 to build a capitol building and penitentiary, the general assembly voted to move the state government to the banks of the Scioto River. In 1816, 13 years after Ohio became a state, Columbus became its capital.

The Statehouse is where our laws are made; inside the top of the Statehouse rotunda is the Ohio State Seal, created in stained glass.

The red carnation became Ohio's state flower in honor of Ohioan president, William McKinley. One day a friend offered him a bright red carnation to wear in his lapel for good luck, and it must have worked, because from that day on, he always wore the flower. In fact, thanks to his friend's beautiful carnation beds in Alliance, that town became know as Carnation City.

Ohio's state bird is the cardinal, a North American songbird that lives in Ohio all year. Male cardinals can grow to be 9 inches long and are dressed in bright red suits with a crest on their heads and a thick orange-red bill. The females are reddish-brown.

In Ohio many symbols and places start with the letter C, and none could be more important than Columbus, our capital city.

In May, the rare and beautiful Lakeside Daisy blooms along Lake Erie's shore on the Marblehead Peninsula, which is the only place in the United States where the plant grows naturally. The yellow Lakeside Daisy has become the rarest of all endangered plants in Ohio.

Daisy is also one of the oldest and most common name for a dairy cow—perhaps because cows often graze in fields of daisies. Dairy products like milk, cream, and cheese are among Ohio's leading agricultural products, thanks to the thriving dairy farms here. In 1880, the huge production of milk and the 40 cheese factories near Wellington prompted the town to be christened the "Cheese Capital of the United States."

D can be for Dairy cow
in fields grazing
and for Ohio's wildflower
the yellow Lakeside Daisy.

In 1669, French explorer Louis Joliet discovered Lake Erie and for the next 100 years France and England argued about who owned it. The fourth largest of the Great Lakes, Lake Erie is also the shallowest. Its 9,940 square miles separate Ontario, Canada from the United States. Lake Erie is 241 miles long, between 30 and 57 miles wide, and as deep as 210 feet. More than 300 bird species nest in the woods and marshes along the shore and many varieties of wildflowers, mammals, reptiles, and amphibians also make their homes here. Lake Erie has more numbers and varieties of fish than any of the other Great Lakes.

U.S. Naval Officer Oliver Hazard Perry built and manned a fleet of ships on Lake Erie during the War of 1812 that was fought between the United States and Great Britain. The Battle of Lake Erie has been called the most decisive naval battle in history and the biggest battle ever fought on inland waters. In September 1813, near Put-in-Bay, Ohio, Commodore Perry forced the British navy to surrender the entire lake to the United States. His report of the battle became one of history's most famous phrases: "We have met the enemy and they are ours."

The letter E stands for Erie,
a lake that's great fun to explore.
Rocks and sandy beaches have secrets galore
and long ago, battles were once seen offshore.

F is for Flint,
a rock with powers that early man could mint.
Fire and firearms were made with Ohio's gemstone.
So were arrowheads and tools, the earliest ones known.

Flint is Ohio's official gemstone and is the darkest variety of chert, a type of quartz. The stone was first used 15,000 years ago to make knives and spearheads because, although it is very hard, it can easily be shaped by flaking off the edges with a blunt rock or small hammer. Before matches were invented, people would hit steel against flint to strike a spark that would light fires. Gun makers in the seventeenth and eighteenth centuries combined flint and steel to set off the gunpowder in the flintlock guns used by America's early pioneers.

Flint Ridge State Memorial and Museum in Newark preserves pit areas where American Indians once mined flint. The museum traces the mineral from its raw state to its many uses by Native Americans.

Ff

Glacier starts with the letter G.
Made of ice and snow,
it carved hills and valleys
millions of years ago.

Glaciers created Ohio's many different land formations long before men, women, and children lived on earth. A glacier is a mass of ice formed in high mountains and polar regions. When the snow is compressed it begins to move by the pressure of its own weight. Millions of years ago, the Wisconsin Glacier moved across what would become Ohio, carving gorges, ravines, rock bridges, huge boulders, cliffs, and recessed caves into the landscape. It also formed waterfalls and smoothed the land in northwestern Ohio into flat plains.

Within the 800 acres of Kelleys Island State Park are glacial grooves, where fossilized marine life is embedded in limestone bedrock. These grooves are considered among the finest glacial carvings in America.

H is the letter for this special place
full of butterflies, squirrels, and bees.
Holden Arboretum is nature's delight
with gardens of flowers, plants, and trees.

Arboretum is another word for botanical garden, a public place where plants are grown for people to enjoy and for scientists to study. Arbor is the Latin word for tree, so an arboretum concentrates on woody plants, trees, and shrubs.

The largest arboretum in the United States is located in northeastern Ohio. Holden Arboretum, covering 3,100 acres, has miles of walking trails that weave through its woodland "museum" passing woods, lakes, fields, and ravines. Look for rhododendrons, lilacs, buckeyes, and crab apples along with maples, evergreens, and wildflowers. There is a white oak tree in Holden Arboretum that is more than 350 years old.

Ohio is—and has been—the home of many inventors. Wilbur and Orville Wright invented an airplane that would fly. W.F. Semple patented chewing gum in 1869. Engineer Charles Kettering held 140 patents for his inventions, among them an electric starter that helped in the development of the modern automobile. Granville Woods is sometimes called "Ohio's Forgotten Inventor." He patented more than 50 inventions, including automatic railroad brakes and other electrical devices that made railroads safer.

Many of Ohio's inventors worked on lights. Garrett Morgan invented the first traffic light. Charles Brush created the electric arc light, which replaced earlier gas streetlights. Thomas Edison made an even better electric light. Later, Arthur Compton invented the skinny florescent light tubes we use in schools and homes.

Ii

I is for Inventors,
people who use their imagination.
Their job is to think of something new,
like airplanes, lights, and chewing gum too.

J stands for John Chapman,
  a man who sowed seeds and did good deeds.
 Early settlers all agreed
that he deserved the name, Johnny Appleseed.

Johnny Appleseed is one of the best-loved characters in American history and folklore. He was born in Massachusetts in 1774 and was named Johnny Chapman. For 40 years he wandered throughout western Pennsylvania, Ohio, and Indiana, sowing apple seeds that in time grew into orchards enjoyed by pioneers. Legends say that Johnny Appleseed wore his cooking pot on his head as he traveled. In 1840, even though John Chapman settled in a cabin near Mansfield, he continued to wander for hundreds of miles planting apple seeds. Stories about his love of animals and great kindness spread far and wide and he became a legend in his own day. He died in 1845, but a few of the trees he planted still grow in Ohio. He was living proof of his motto: "The good that men do lives after them."

Jj

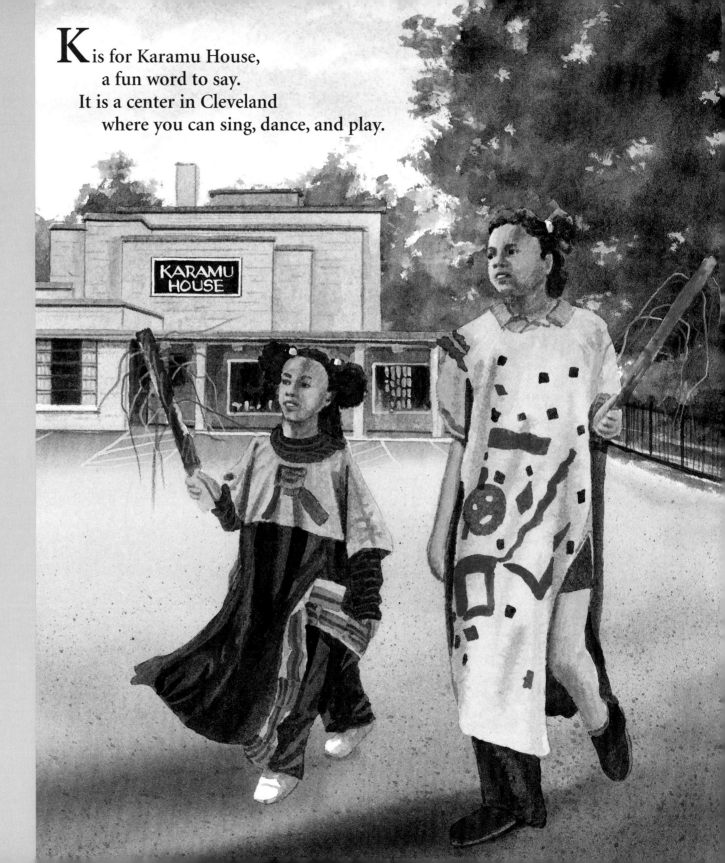

K is for Karamu House,
a fun word to say.
It is a center in Cleveland
where you can sing, dance, and play.

Karamu is a word that means "a place of joyful gatherings" in the Swahili language. The Karamu House in Cleveland is the oldest African-American cultural arts center in the United States. It was founded in 1915 by two graduates of Ohio's Oberlin College, our nation's first coeducational interracial college. Russell and Rowena Woodham Jelliffe wanted to bring people of different backgrounds, races, and religions together to develop their artistic talents. Inside the Karamu House there are theaters, dance and art studios, an art gallery, an early childhood development center, and even a neighborhood bank.

The ladybug, sometimes called a Ladybird Beetle, is Ohio's state insect. Less than a quarter-inch long and round in shape, ladybugs have tiny wings and short legs. Some have red or yellow backs that are covered with black spots. Others have black backs with yellow or red spots. These helpful beetles eat destructive plant-eating insects. They have big appetites and big families, so scientists often call upon them to help stop nature's pests from eating crops and vegetation.

Now we have a special insect
hiding in our book.
What can it be?
Come and take a look!

L stands for Ladybug.
Tiny, red and black,
    she wears a cloak of polka dots
        upon her round, hard back.

Named for Queen Marie Antoinette of France, Marietta sits where the Muskingum and Ohio rivers meet. Marietta became the first capital of the Northwest Territory. During its early years, many paddleboats moved along the two rivers, ferrying goods and settlers. Several boats in town can be toured.

mM

M is for Marietta,
    a charming river town
        where crowds gather, bands play,
            and paddle wheels go round and round.

N stands for Nature,
living things in the great outdoors
such as Ohio's prairies and pine forests
as well as scenic lakeshores.

Nature preserves may look like parks, but they are designed and maintained for visitors who fly in with wings or visit on four paws, hooves, or feet. The Ohio Department of Natural Resources protects many of these special areas and asks human visitors to help.

Some nature preserves have unusual rock formations. In Rockbridge State Nature Preserve, a 100-foot rock bridge was formed more than a million years ago. Ohio caverns display pure white stalactites and stalagmites against a backdrop of vividly colored walls. Hocking Hills State Park has recess caves and waterfalls, gorges, rock pools, winding ravines, and other natural formations.

The white-tailed deer, Ohio's state mammal, can be found in all of Ohio's 88 counties. When frightened the white-tailed deer raises its tail, which is white on the underside, as a flag warning family members of possible danger. Fawns recognize their mothers by sniffing the scent glands on their ankles.

Pulitzer Prize winner and Ohio native Louis Bromfield once pointed out, "Ohio is the farthest West of the East and the farthest North of the South."

The name comes from the Iroquois word *Oheyo*, which means "beautiful river" or "great river," and it is indeed a state with many beautiful rivers, as well as rolling pastures, prairies, plateaus, forests, and rocky cliffs.

For centuries, Native American tribes roamed the area. At the end of the French and Indian War in 1763, Great Britain acquired the land and held it until the end of the American Revolution. Once claimed by both Connecticut and Virginia, Ohio became part of the Northwest Territory in 1787. Eventually the area was separated, and in 1803, Ohio was admitted to the Union as the 17th state.

The earliest settlers left their homes in New England, Pennsylvania, Kentucky, and Virginia to move to Ohio. In the 1830s, the German and Swiss arrived. In the 1840s, the Irish followed. The flourishing Amish and Mennonite communities have also helped make Ohio a unique place to live.

O! This one is tricky! See if you can guess:
What's round on the ends and "hi" in the middle?

The answer is OHIO!
Did you figure out the riddle?

Warren G. Harding

William H. Harrison

Ulysses S. Grant

William H. Taft

From Ohio came eight Presidents,
bringing us to the letter **P**.
Two Harrisons, one Hayes,
a Grant and a Garfield,
portly Taft, Harding, and a
carnation-clad McKinley.

Rutherford B. Hayes

William McKinley

Benjamin Harrison

James A. Garfield

Ohio is known as "The Mother of Presidents" because it has sent more men to the White House than any other state. The first president from Ohio was our 9th president, William Henry Harrison (1773-1841). A general during the War of 1812, he won the presidency in 1840.

The 18th president, Ulysses S. Grant (1822-1885) commanded the Union armies during the Civil War.

Rutherford B. Hayes (1822-1893) followed Grant in office, becoming the 19th president.

James A. Garfield (1831-1881) was the 20th president. He was assassinated four months after taking office.

The grandson of William Henry Harrison, Benjamin Harrison (1833-1901) became the 23rd president.

Our 25th president, William McKinley (1843-1901), was a former governor of Ohio before being elected president in 1896. He was assassinated, in Buffalo, during his second term.

William Howard Taft (1857-1930), was the only president to become Chief Justice of the Supreme Court. Taft was elected our 27th president in 1908.

Warren G. Harding (1865-1923), our 29th president of the United States, ran for office in 1921 with the promise to return the country to "normalcy" (a word he made up) after World War I.

Q stands for Quaker Oats,
Ohio's favorite breakfast food.
Steaming hot and swimming in milk,
it puts us in a happy mood.

The forerunner of the Quaker Oats Company began in Akron in 1854 by Ferdinand Schumacher, a German immigrant who in time became known as the "Cereal King of America." In 1872, he established the Empire Barley Mill in Akron. Eleven years later, he built an eight-story jumbo mill that covered an entire city block. A devastating fire in 1886 led to a merger with the Akron Milling Company. Then, in 1901, it became a major component of the Quaker Oats Company.

Quaker Oats stopped production in Akron in 1970 and the headquarters moved. Today the 36 huge grain silos are part of the Quaker Square Hilton Hotel, where the silos no longer store oats, wheat, and barley, but rather house 186 rooms for hotel guests. Nearby, a 1938 Broadway Limited train, once used to transport grain to the milling company, displays a collection of railroad memorabilia.

The largest collection of roller coasters in the world can be found at Cedar Point in Sandusky. The 364-acre amusement park opened in 1870 and today has 14 roller coasters. During the first year of the new millennium, Millennium Force opened, a 310-foot high world-record-breaking roller coaster offering a 92-mile-an-hour fright. Cedar Point also has the tallest free-fall ride in the world (the Power Tower with a 300-foot drop) and has 68 amusement rides, the most in one park. There are more than 2,000 trash cans to keep the park clean!

R rolls over the tongue
like a Roller coaster over its rails.
With breathtaking dives
and high-speed glides,
roller coasters give
the most rollicking rides.

Rr

S stands for Columbus's ship, the *Santa Maria*.
In Fourteen Hundred and Ninety-Two,
  she left Spain and sailed the ocean blue
   with a fearless captain and a valiant crew.

Ss

Because Columbus was named for explorer Christopher Columbus, in honor of the 500th anniversary of Columbus's trip to America, the mayor of the city commissioned the building of a replica of the explorer's flagship, the *Santa Maria*. It is a wooden ship with three masts and five large sails. Like the original *Santa Maria*, the replica is 98 feet long. Opened for tours in 1992, the *Santa Maria* replica is permanently moored downtown on the Scioto River at Battelle Park.

T is for Tomato
which makes the beverage of Ohio.
Here, tons of tasty tomatoes grow
to produce the juice Ohioans know.

Tomato juice was adopted as the state beverage in 1965. Ohio leads the country in the production of tomato juice and is second only to California in the number of tomatoes grown each summer.

The tomato is actually classified as the fruit of an herb plant in the nightshade family. Before the nineteenth century, settlers believed that the tomato was poisonous and often called it the "love apple." There are many varieties of tomatoes, whose plants produce round or oval fruit that turns either yellow or red when ripe.

The Underground Railroad was not a real train that ran on railroad tracks, but a transportation system made of people helping people. Established before the Civil War when slavery existed in the southern states, the Underground Railroad transported slaves to freedom. Many secret paths wound through the countryside, starting at the Ohio River and curving north to Lake Erie. A candle in a window or a gourd beside a door would indicate that help and food awaited the runaways. These safe houses were called "stations" and the brave Ohioans who helped slaves were known as "conductors." Slaves were not free until they reached Canada on the other side of Lake Erie.

Ohio has many historic sites where slaves stayed; among them are the 1840s Hubbard House in Ashtabula and the Rankin House in Ripley.

Many famous Ohioans fought to free the slaves. Harriet Beecher Stowe of Cincinnati battled slavery with her pen when she wrote *Uncle Tom's Cabin*. The Union's most effective Civil War generals—Ulysses S. Grant, William Tecumseh Sherman, Philip Sheridan, and George Armstrong Custer—were all Ohioans.

Underground Railroad starts with **U**.
It had no train, no engine,
no whistle that blew.
Hidden "stations" marked by secret clues
and kind "conductors" led slaves
to safe houses they knew.

James Murray Spangler of Canton was a janitor with a brilliant idea. In his day, carpet sweepers were manual, not electric, but he knew electricity would create possibilities for labor-saving devices. In 1907, Spangler built an electric suction sweeper using metal, wood, and a pillowcase as a bag to capture the dirt. After having his invention patented, he sold it to a businessman named William Hoover. Hoover worked from Spangler's prototype and manufactured the first successful portable electric suction sweeper in 1908. In time, the Electric Suction Sweeper Company of New Berlin (now North Canton) became the Hoover Company. Hoover still makes vacuum cleaners, as well as rug cleaners and other floor care items.

Vacuum cleaner begins with V
a favorite for those who go on a cleaning spree.
Push it around after you turn it on
and very soon the dirt is gone.

Aviation pioneers Wilbur and Orville Wright were brothers living in Dayton shortly after the Civil War. In the 1890s, they started manufacturing bicycles, studying aeronautical literature, and experimenting with gliders to learn wind control and lateral balancing. They tested their gliders at Kitty Hawk, N.C., where the winds were known to be fairly constant. On December 17, 1903, Orville made the first flight in a power-driven plane, but the world knew nothing of those 12 precious seconds or the brothers' work until five years later, when a newspaper reporter named D. Bruce Salley witnessed their 1,000-foot flight.

Dayton, the birthplace of aviation, was the Wright brothers' home and the site of the Wright Cycle Company Shop. Nearby, at Huffman Prairie, the Wrights built and tested some of their "flying machines." A memorial and replica of their hangar can be found there today.

W is for Wright brothers
who dreamt of reaching the sky,
they built planes in their bicycle shop
and became the first inventors to fly.

Once the site of the Shawnee Nations' largest settlement, Xenia is the birthplace of Shawnee Chief Tecumseh. He and his brother, The Prophet, united western Indians to protect their tribal lands and culture from encroaching frontiersmen. Tecumseh was defeated at the Battle of Tippecanoe, where another Ohioan, William Henry Harrison, commanded United States troops. Later Harrison became our 9th president. Another Ohio general, William Tecumseh Sherman, was named for the chief known to be brave in battle.

Xenia is known as the City of Hospitality because its name in Greek means hospitality. It is also known as Trail City USA, after being ranked as one of the best cities in the U.S. to hike, bike, and skate. The trails follow the path of old railroad tracks.

The X word is Xenia
though its X sounds like a Z.
This is Ohio's City of Hospitality
it's also a great place to bike—try it and see.

Y y

The Y bridge spans two rivers
keeping travelers dry.
You can cross the bridge and not the river
though you may be wondering why.

Zanesville sits at the junction of two scenic highways and two rivers, the Muskingum and the Licking. Since 1814, five different bridges have been constructed at the same location over these rivers. The fifth bridge boasts one of the world's most unusual designs. On this three-way overpass, you can indeed cross the bridge without crossing a river. West Main Street, Linden Avenue, and U.S. 40 meet in the middle of the bridge. The best view of this unusual structure is from Putnam Hill Park Overlook.

Ohio has five zoos: Toledo Zoo, Akron Zoological Park, Cleveland Metroparks Zoo, Columbus Zoo, and the Cincinnati Zoo and Botanical Garden. Each provides homes for rare and wonderful creatures from every corner of the world.

The Toledo Zoo was the first zoo in the world to design a "hippoquarium" where visitors can watch the hippos swimming underwater in their see-through tank. It also features a savanna area and a 17,000-square-foot gorilla meadow. At the Columbus and Cincinnati zoos you can see the endangered manatee in specially designed aquariums.

Zz

Z stands for Zoo,
where hippos and manatees are on view.
Visitors can watch alligators chew,
and rare red pandas will wave at you.

Now we've said the ABCs
it is fun as fun can be
and we've discovered Ohio
from the letters A to Z!

A Basket of Buckeye Facts

1. Do you know Ohio's state motto?

2. During the Civil War, only one battle was fought in Ohio. Can you name it? (Hint: It was fought in and along the Ohio River.)

3. In this same battle, three officers who fought together would one day become presidents of the United States. Who are these Ohio presidents?

4. What president from Ohio served the shortest term?

5. Who was our nation's "First Lady?" (Hint: It wasn't Martha Washington.)

6. How many counties are there in Ohio?

7. We learned that Ohio's state flower is the carnation. Do you know the name of our state wildflower? How many petals does it have?

8. What is the highest place in Ohio?

9. Ohio became a state in 1803. How many states did that make?

10. What is the capital of Ohio? Now, where were the earlier capital cities?

11. Ohio has many words taken from the Native Americans who lived here. Can you name the seven settlements who lived here before the Europeans arrived?

12. Which of the Great Lakes is the shallowest?

13. Ohio has a rock song. What is the name of it and what university band made it popular?

14. What is Ohio's state reptile?

15. What does the sun rising above the mountains on "Great Seal of Ohio" stand for? What does the wheat symbolize?

16. What is Ohio's state fossil?

17. Where was the War of 1812 fought in Ohio?

18. An African American from Cleveland, Ohio, Garrett Morgan invented something that made traffic flow more smoothly. Do you know what he invented? (Hint: You probably see at least one every day.)

19. Two bodies of water border Ohio. What are they?

20. What and where is the largest military museum in the world?

Answers:

1. "With God, all things are possible."

2. The Battle of Buffington Island.

3. Rutherford B. Hayes, James Garfield, and William McKinley

4. William Henry Harrison served only 32 days.

5. It was the Lucy Webb Hayes, wife of Rutherford B. Hayes, our 19th president. She was called the "First Lady" by a reporter and the befitting title for presidential wives stuck ever since. She was also the first First Lady to have a college diploma. She graduated from Ohio Wesleyan Women's College in 1850.

6. 88.

7. Our state wildflower, the White Trillium, has three petals.

8. Campbell Hill, near Bellefontaine, Ohio, is the highest point between the Appalachian Mountains and the Mississippi River. It is 1,550 feet above sea level.

9. Ohio became the 17th state.

10. Columbus is the capital. Marietta, Cincinnati, Chillicothe and Zanesville all served as capitals until 1816.

11. Ottawa, Wyandot, Erie, Tuscarora, Miami, Shawnee, and Delaware.

12. Lake Erie.

13. A band in Dayton wrote "Hang on Sloopy," but The Ohio State University Marching Band made it popular in the 1960s and continues to play it each season.

14. The Black Racer Snake, because it can be found in each county.

15. The sun represents Ohio, as the first state west of the Allegheny Mountains. The wheat reminds us of the importance of agriculture in Ohio.

16. It is the trilobite. It is an extinct sea creature that lived in Ohio 440 million years ago when the state was covered with salt water.

17. On Lake Erie. Commodore Oliver Hazard Perry and his American fleet defeated the British near South Bass Island. Today, Perry's Victory and International Peace Memorial salutes the win and also our friendship with Canada which shares Lake Erie as a border.

18. Garrett Morgan invented the traffic light in 1923.

19. Lake Erie on the North and the Ohio River on the South.

20. The United States Air Force Museum in Dayton.

Cardinal Numbers

An Ohio Counting Book

To Cullen —

You can count on Ohio!

Marcia Schonberg

Written by Marcia Schonberg and Illustrated by Bruce Langton

Sleeping Bear Press
310 North Main Street
P.O. Box 20
Chelsea, MI 48118
www.sleepingbearpress.com

Printed and bound in China.

10 9 8 7 6 5 4 3 2 1

Library of Congress Cataloging-in-Publication Data
Schonberg, Marcia.
Cardinal numbers : an Ohio counting book / author, Marcia Schonberg ;
illustrator, Bruce Langton.
p. cm.
Summary: Presents short rhymes about numbers of objects from one through fourteen
and provides information about the Ohio natural history and social studies topics that
the objects represent. Also includes a set of open-ended counting problems.
ISBN 1-58536-084-8
1. Counting-Juvenile literature. 2. Ohio-Description and travel-Juvenile literature.
[1. Counting. 2. Ohio.] I. Langton, Bruce, ill. II. Title.
QA113 .S387 2002
[E]—dc21
2002007344

Cardinal Numbers *is about the numbers we find in Ohio*
and ones we use each day. Special thanks to educators Lisa Shambaugh,
Karen Higgins, and Grace Sunbury for their professional suggestions.
They dedicate themselves to making teaching and learning a personal,
creative, and meaningful experience—like the ones you can gather
along with the buckeyes within these pages.

To Brandon and Joel whose smiles bring me countless amounts of joy each day.

To Bill who's always been "Number 1" to me.

M.S.

This book is dedicated to all the wonderful children that
have touched my heart throughout my life.

To Rebecca, Brett, and Rory... Without you my life would not be the same.
Thank you for just being there.

Lastly, my thanks to Sleeping Bear Press and Marcia Schonberg for
all their hard work and dedication on such a wonderful book.

B.L.

There are tiny buckeyes
hiding in our book.
Maybe 1 on every page.
Take a careful look.

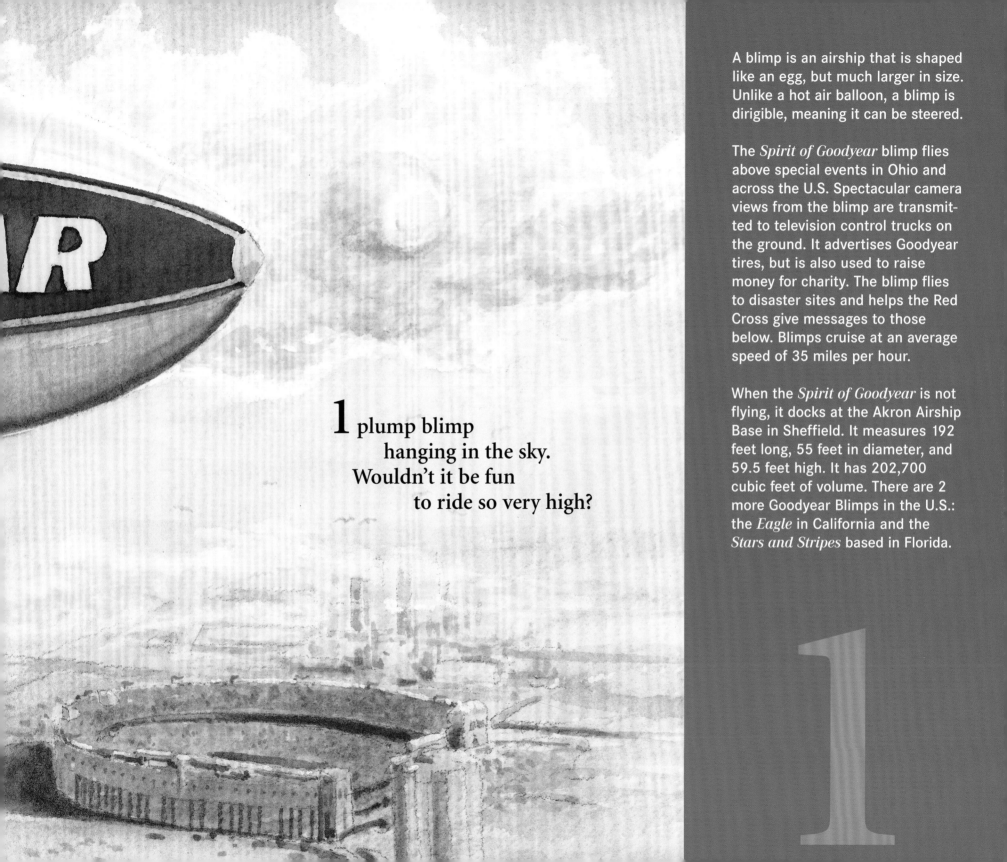

1 plump blimp
    hanging in the sky.
Wouldn't it be fun
    to ride so very high?

A blimp is an airship that is shaped like an egg, but much larger in size. Unlike a hot air balloon, a blimp is dirigible, meaning it can be steered.

The *Spirit of Goodyear* blimp flies above special events in Ohio and across the U.S. Spectacular camera views from the blimp are transmitted to television control trucks on the ground. It advertises Goodyear tires, but is also used to raise money for charity. The blimp flies to disaster sites and helps the Red Cross give messages to those below. Blimps cruise at an average speed of 35 miles per hour.

When the *Spirit of Goodyear* is not flying, it docks at the Akron Airship Base in Sheffield. It measures 192 feet long, 55 feet in diameter, and 59.5 feet high. It has 202,700 cubic feet of volume. There are 2 more Goodyear Blimps in the U.S.: the *Eagle* in California and the *Stars and Stripes* based in Florida.

Ohio immigrants began building canals to connect Lake Erie with the Ohio River. The first segment of the Ohio and Erie Canal was completed between Cleveland and Akron in 1827. It took 7 years to dig the entire 309-mile-long canal by hand. Workers made sure the canals were 4 feet deep and wide enough for 2 boats traveling in opposite directions to pass. Locks raised and lowered the water level to maintain the depth. Approximately 1,000 miles of canals were built in Ohio between 1825 and 1847.

Teams of mules or workhorses followed the towpath, a narrow trail along side the canal, as they pulled the boats. Many of these old paths are popular multiuse bikeways today.

Canal boats traveled 2 to 4 miles an hour. The cost for a boat trip varied depending on the distance traveled, but passengers usually paid 2 to 5 cents per mile to travel on a canal boat.

2

Before fast cars and trains
canal boats were fun to ride.
Slowly, they were towed
by 2 horses, side by side.

The white trillium is Ohio's state wildflower. It has 3 petals, 3 sepals, and 3 leaves. The white trillium turns pink as it gets older. Wildflowers first appear in early spring when the daylight increases and there is more sunlight. The southwestern part of Ohio sees the first blooms in early April. There are 2,300 species of wild-flowers in Ohio.

3

Count the petals,
1, 2, 3.
Now count white trillium.
How many do you see?

Can you find the Canada goose
guarding the river's shore?
Then find fluffy yellow goslings
lined up in rows of 4.

Canada geese migrate to Ohio, but Giant Canada geese live here year-round. They mate for life. That is why the gander helps the female protect their young goslings each spring. Identify Canada geese by the white patches that look like chin straps below their short bills. Listen for their distinctive honks. Look for their V-shape during flight. You will see them in Ohio's lakes and streams.

Ohio has more than 60,000 miles of streams. An average of 38 inches of water from rain, ice, hail, and snow feed Ohio streams every year. Streams in the northern third of Ohio flow into Lake Erie. From Lake Erie the water flows into the Atlantic Ocean by way of Lake Ontario and the St. Lawrence Seaway.

Streams more than 100 miles long are called rivers. The Muskingum, Scioto, and Great Miami are just a few of the rivers that flow south to their final destination in the Gulf of Mexico.

4

Paddling **5** canoes,
   beneath the summer sun.
On Ohio's rivers,
   what could be more fun?

Ohio's rivers are fun places and there's no better way to explore them than by canoe. Put on a life jacket and learn how to paddle a canoe. You can travel along many streams including the 11 special river systems that are part of the Ohio State Scenic Rivers System.

Streams in Ohio are home to fish and many other forms of life. If you go fishing, the first thing you must learn is to have patience. While you are waiting for a fish, look for dragonflies as they dart above the water or go below. There are many species of turtles and snakes living in Ohio streams too. Listen for bullfrogs that say *jug-o-rum, jug-o-rum* and green frogs that call out a *twang* sound. Maybe you will see a salamander, an amphibian with a tail.

5

The black racer snake was named the state reptile in 1995 because racers are found in each of Ohio's 88 counties. This snake eats small rodents such as mice so farmers consider it a friend. Its scientific name is *Coluber constrictor*, but it is not a constrictor. There are 2 kinds of racer snakes in Ohio, the black racer and the blue racer. They are called *racer* because they can move up to speeds of 8-10 miles per hour. The largest snake in Ohio is the black rat snake. It can grow to 8 feet in length.

Racer snakes are predators. Because they eat mice and rats, racers help farmers control the rodent population. About 46 different species and subspecies of snakes make their home in Ohio's natural areas.

6 black racer snakes
hiding near the barn.
They may slither and surprise you,
but they are helpers on the farm.

GENERAL STORE

Drive down country roads,
looking all around.
Count 7 Amish buggies,
hitched in an Amish town.

Amish and Mennonite people love the land and like to farm, but they also enjoy creating beautiful hand-made quilts and furniture. Most of them immigrated from Switzerland searching for religious freedom. They were called Anabaptists. Ohio's counties of Holmes, Wayne, Tuscarawas, and Stark have the greatest Amish population (about 35,000) in the world. Some also live in Geauga County.

The Amish do not drive automobiles or use electricity. Businesses in Amish communities have hitching posts for horse and buggies, and parking lots for non-Amish drivers. Do you know one way to tell if a farmhouse is Amish? You won't see any electrical wires or telephone poles. They believe in living simply without modern conveniences, but they have fun and enjoy themselves like everyone else. It is against their religious teachings to be photo-graphed so please respect their wishes when you visit.

7

Ohio is 1 of 7 states to name the cardinal as its official state bird. It is the most popular of all state birds and became Ohio's favorite in 1933. The cardinal does not migrate—it stays all winter. It munches sun-flower seeds at backyard feeders. It also eats other seeds, berries, and insects. Both the male and female have a crest (a tuft of feathers atop their head), long tail, and red bill, but the male is the beautiful bright red bird we easily identify. The feathers on a female and young cardinal are camouflage colors of light brown.

8

Bright red cardinals
bring us to number 8.
Look very closely.
Can you match each with a mate?

9 Longaberger baskets
    handmade in many shapes.
Filled with Ohio foods—
    tomatoes, corn, and grapes.

Visitors come from all over the U.S. to see the world's largest basket in Dresden. It is woven from strips of maple and measures 48 feet long. In the Longaberger factories, artisans weave more baskets than anywhere else in the United States.

Half of Ohio's land is considered prime farmland. Only 3 other states have such high percentages of fertile land as Ohio. Farmers in Ohio grow food for people all over the world. They put Ohio in the top 10 for harvesting tomatoes, corn, and grapes as well as other farm products like soybeans, oats, and wheat.

9

In 1912, when candy maker Clarence Crane created the first Life Saver, mint was the only flavor.

Mr. Crane owned a candy shop in Cleveland. His chocolate candy melted during the hot summer. He knew that most mints imported from Europe were square and individually wrapped and they didn't melt easily. The idea for the round candies came to him one day when he was at the pharmacy. There he saw a pill maker, a device used for making small round pills by hand. He used it to create a round shape and then punched a tiny hole in the middle of each circle. The tiny round shapes reminded him of the life preservers used on ships so he called them Life Savers. He invented them in his hometown of Garrettsville. Today, Life Savers come in 25 flavors.

10

Shiny round Life Savers
are such fun to eat.
Line them up and count to 10
before you taste your treat.

11 hikers in the woods
walking 1 by 1.
Explore the Buckeye Trail—
wouldn't that be fun?

The Buckeye Trail is the longest hiking trail in Ohio. It leads hikers 1,250 miles around the perimeter of the state. Portions of the trail connect to existing roads while other parts follow the towpath of the Ohio-Erie Canal and old railroad beds. You will see forests, parks, and cities if you hike the entire trail. The route is marked by light blue rectangles about 2 X 6 inches in size. These blue blazes guide you along the trail.

There are many other paths to hike in Ohio too. Find one that winds around lakes, streams, or old canal locks, or hike a trail that has hills and valleys. You may even know a trail that follows city streets. Where is your favorite hiking spot?

11

Sugar shack is the term for the building where maple sap is boiled into syrup. Ohio has 800 sugar shacks, some operated by large companies and others by individuals.

Ohio usually produces more maple syrup than any other state except Vermont, New York, and sometimes Pennsylvania. The amount of syrup Ohio produces depends on the weather. The ideal weather for harvesting sap is warm, sunny days followed by cold evenings. It takes 40 gallons of sap to make 1 gallon of syrup. Maple trees are used to collect sap because they are plentiful in the northeast U.S. and have a high concentration of sugar.

Long ago, Native Americans filled hollowed-out logs with sap and added heated rocks to make syrup. Early pioneers cooked their sap outdoors in black pots over an open flame. Today, modern maple syrup producers use evaporators. These devices make 1 to 2 gallons of maple syrup in an hour.

12

Now we have 12 buckets
collecting maple sap.
We'll make sweet syrup
up at the sugar shack.

What hangs on Ohio's state tree
13 hiding in a prickly shell?
Find **13** round buckeyes
Ohioans know so well.

The Ohio buckeye tree has been the official state tree since 1953, but its roots and name go back centuries. Native Americans named the shiny brown nut "hetuck," meaning the eye of a buck or male deer. Pioneers chose buckeye wood for the base logs of their cabins. They believed it resisted insects. Later, William Henry Harrison used the buckeye tree as a symbol during his presidential campaign in 1840.

Today, the state champion buckeye tree grows in North Bend near Cincinnati on land once owned by John Aston Warder, the founding father of the American Forestry Association. While most Ohio buckeye trees grow to 30-50 feet tall, the state champion is 82 feet high and measures 162 inches in circumference. The leafy branches can spread out to 67 feet wide.

13

It takes 3 days to make 1 whistle at the American Whistle Corporation in Columbus. This small factory makes more than 1 million whistles a year and is the only manufacturer of metal whistles in the United States. The whistles made here are the loudest in the world. Police departments, community organizations, schools, the National Football League (NFL), and youth soccer associations purchase them.

Whistles are made of different types of metals from chrome and brass to 24-karat gold plate. People who work outdoors in winter buy rubber Safe-T-Tips for their whistles to keep their lips from sticking to the cold metal.

14

14 shiny metal whistles
make the shrillest sound.
In a game or traffic jam,
a whistle can be found.

Author's note: The following problems reflect a creative and open-ended approach to mathematics. Answers, while not always specific, encourage discussion, divergent thinking and dialogue among children and between children and adults.

Classroom teachers across the grade levels and state encouraged me as I created the remaining pages. They serve as a starting point—one that, hopefully, will lead to the wonderment of self-discovery. Please use any of the numbers and topics in *Cardinal Numbers* to help your child acquire number concepts while learning about themselves and the state of Ohio.

Most of all, I hope you have as much fun sharing these "buckeye" numbers as I had in writing them.

—M.S.

We've counted Ohio numbers,
starting with number 1.
Now use your imagination.
It's time to have more fun.

You'll find clues in these pages
and sometimes answers, too.
But discovering possibilities
is what we each must do.

Problem 1:

The size of the Goodyear blimp
is 192 feet.
Is it bigger than your room?
Or a house on your street?

Problem 2:

Arrange 192
in groups that are smaller.
100s, 10s and 1s.
Now, isn't that much easier?

Buckeye nuts are not always brown and shiny. The nut is white before it ripens. Folklore says that half of the nut is poisonous and that squirrels know which half is safe to eat. More likely, the nut is so bitter that squirrels stop before the whole nut is eaten.

Problem 3:

Picking up buckeyes
1 handful at a time.
Can you hold 2, 4, or 6?
Now, how many can you find?

Problem 4:

How wide is a buckeye?
   Measure it to see.
      If you make a buckeye necklace,
         how long will it be?

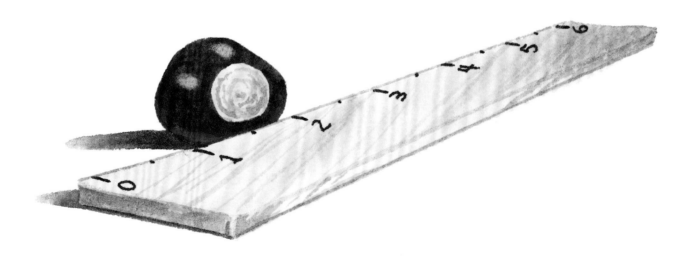

Here are rural counting facts
    to learn what farmers grow.
Ohio farms lead the world.
            Just do the work below.

Problem 5:

Swiss cheese cut in yellow cubes.
            How many do we have?
Please count them all.
            Now count just half.

Problem 6:

Dad bought a dozen eggs
    for his hungry family of 4.
        Each person ate 3 scrambled eggs.
            Could anyone have more?

Ohio produces more Swiss cheese than any other state.

Ohio chickens lay a lot of eggs. In 2001, Ohio cluckers produced 7.9 billion eggs, making it the second largest egg producer in the country. Ohio is second because Iowa has more chickens.

Ohio ranks number 1 in the variety of apples grown in the U.S. Some well-known Ohio apples are Golden Delicious, Red Delicious, Jonathon, Melrose, and Stayman. Specialty varieties like Fuji, Gala, and Granny Smith are increasing in popularity, but are not as plentiful as others. Which apple is your favorite?

Problem 7:

Mmm. Mom's making apple crisp.
Count the apples she will need.
Is the pan round or square?
How many kids will she feed?

Problem 8:

Sweet syrup with breakfast.
How much do you pour?
How many servings in a gallon?
When will you need more?

Ohio is the 7th most populated state of all 50. Can you make a fraction that explains this fact?

It is 205 miles wide and 230 miles long at its farthest points. It has 88 counties. The largest county is Ashtabula in the northeast corner of the state. Right next to it is Lake County, our smallest. The highest point in Ohio is at Campbell Hill, near Bellefontaine. At 1,550 feet above sea level, it is the highest spot between the Appalachian Mountains and the Mississippi River. The lowest point in Ohio is along the Ohio River, near Cincinnati, at 455 feet above sea level.

Problem 9:

Ohio is just 1 state—
    there are 50 in all.
  We think our state is big
    until we make a fraction and then it seems so small.

Problem 10:

How large is Ohio? (44,828 square miles)
      How many people live in our state? (11,353,140 in 2000)
    Now use your calculator—
         how many people per square mile does that make?

We've learned our numbers.
Found many buckeyes too.
Ohio has more math to do,
but now it's up to you—because our book's all through.

Marcia Schonberg

Ohio native and award-winning journalist Marcia Schonberg is a frequent contributor to the *Columbus Dispatch* and a variety of national publications. Her articles and travel guides also appear on the worldwide web. She is the author of Ohio travel guides. Marcia is an active member of the Ohioana Library Association, American Society of Journalists and Authors, Midwest Travel Writers Association, and the Society of Children's Book Writers and Illustrators. She lives with her husband, Bill, in Lexington, Ohio.

Bruce Langton

Bruce Langton is considered a premier contemporary artist. His unmistakable style and unique ability to capture not only sporting and wildlife scenes, but also landscapes has won him numerous national awards and international recognition. Bruce travels nationwide to make interactive presentations to schools and libraries about illustrating children's books.

With over one hundred limited edition prints and etchings on the market, Bruce is now proud to add children's books to his list of achievements: *B is for Buckeye: An Ohio Alphabet*, *V is for Volunteer: A Tennessee Alphabet*, *H is for Hoosier: An Indiana Alphabet*, and *Cardinal Numbers: An Ohio Counting Book*. Bruce resides in Indiana with his wife Rebecca and two sons, Brett and Rory. He enjoys spending time teaching Kyokushinkai karate and teaming as a professional clown with his son Rory.